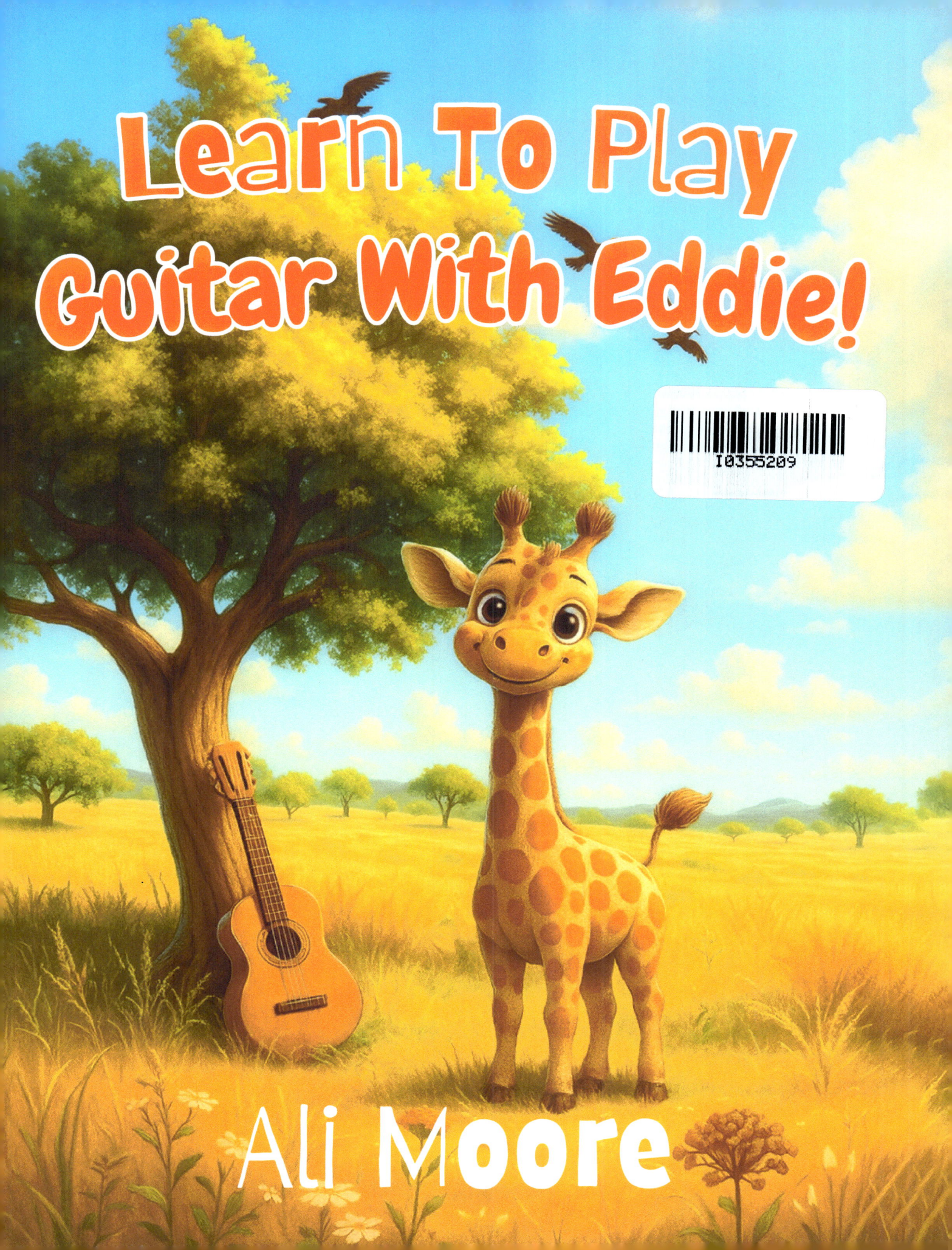

WHEN YOU SEE AN "X" IT MEANS YOU DON'T PLAY THAT STRNIG.

WHEN YOU SEE AN "O" IT MEANS YOU PLAY THAT OPEN STRING.

Eddie Had A Rockin' Jam

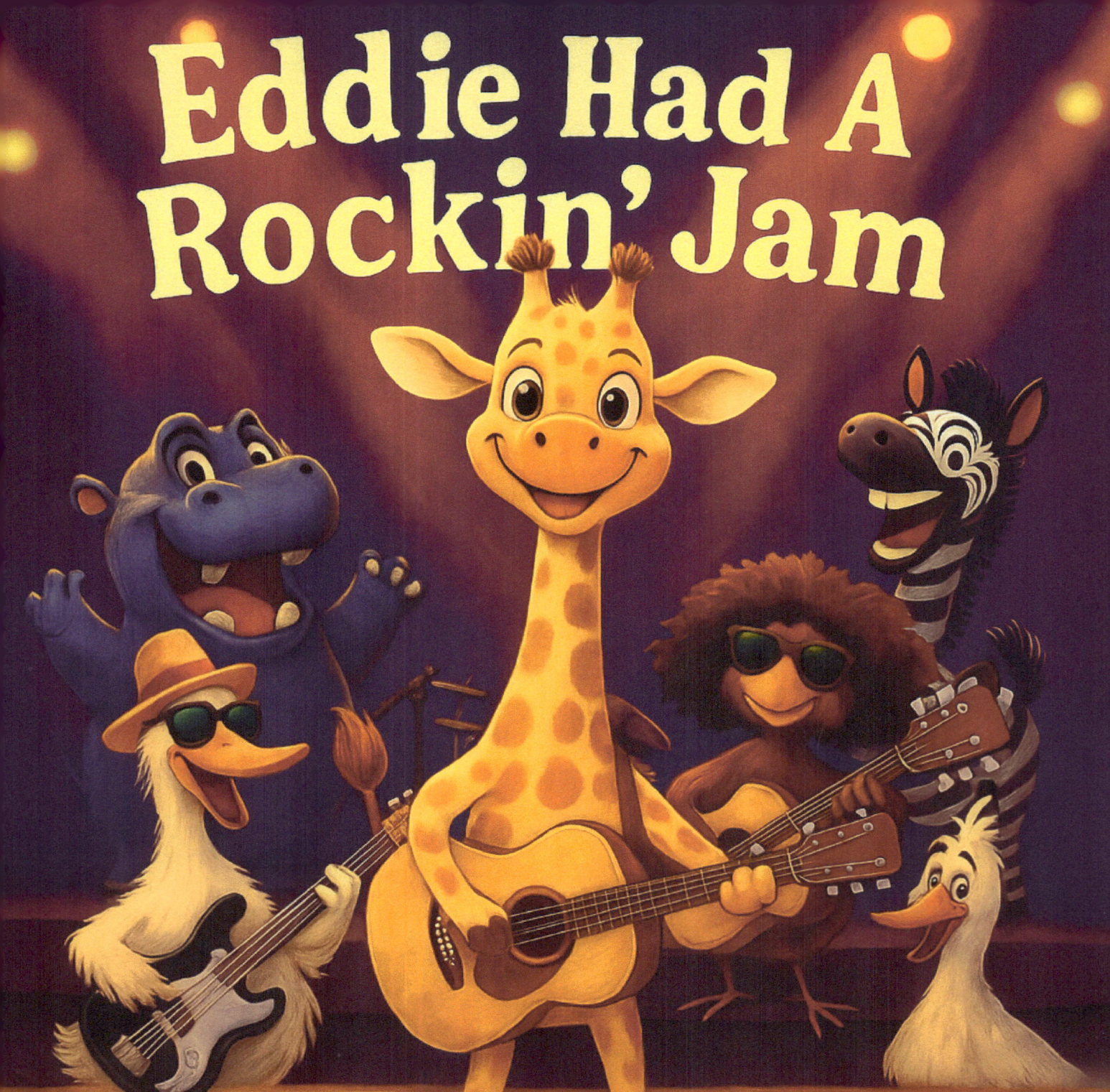

We've learned all about notes, chords, and **TAB**. It's time we put them all into practice!

On the next page is the **TAB** for a new song that Eddie wrote. **"Eddie Had A Rockin' Jam"**. He played it for me earlier, and the tune sounded somewhat familiar. I'm sure it's purely a coincidence and has nothing at all to do with the melody being public domain and free to use... Let me know what you think. Does Eddie's song sound familiar to you?

TAB

"TAB" is short for Tablature, and it's a guitarist's best friend. No, of course you're my best friend, Eddie; it's a figure of speech!

Now, we've talked a little about music notes before. They're part of a special language musicians use to share ideas and bring songs to life. Learning to read music is a fantastic skill, and it's something you should definitely think about as you grow as a musician. But here's a fun fact: Many legendary guitarists couldn't read a single music note, but they still rocked the world! How did they do it? They had help from their (second) best friend—TAB!

TAB is a unique way of writing music that shows you exactly where to put your fingers on the guitar strings. Instead of reading musical pitches like regular sheet music, TAB focuses on the strings and frets you need to play.

It's like a guitar treasure map, guiding you straight to the music without needing to learn the whole musical alphabet. With TAB, even beginners can start playing songs in no time!

CHORD CHARTS

Below is what's known as a chord chart. It's basically a road map to guide you to your chord destination. It tells you which notes to fret, which strings to play, and even which fingers to use! It might as well just play the chord for you!

This is the G Major chord. Eddie has kindly sign-posted every turn on this road sign to G.

ROUTE G MAJOR

FRET

FINGER

STRING

E A D G B E

If you find yourself struggling, I've added a simple version of the G Major chord along with lots of others at the end of this book. Everybody gets to their destination at different speeds. Plus, if we all got there at the same time, it would be awfully crowded! And Eddie doesn't like crowds!

CHORDS

WE'RE GOING TO LEARN ABOUT CHORDS. A CHORD IS A GROUP OF, GENERALLY, THREE OR MORE NOTES PLAYED TOGETHER.

IMAGINE EACH NOTE IS A SUPERHERO, AND WHEN THEY TEAM UP, THEY FORM A SUPERGROUP CALLED A CHORD! TOGETHER, THEY MAKE A BIG, BOLD SOUND THAT'S LIKE A SUPERPOWER IN MUSIC. CHORDS ARE WHAT MAKE SONGS SOUND HAPPY, SAD, OR EVEN EXCITING—A SECRET INGREDIENT TO CREATE MUSICAL MAGIC! ARE YOU READY TO DISCOVER THEIR POWERS?

Let's try playing our first note!

Here's how you can fret (play) a note:

- Make sure your guitar is sitting comfortably in your lap. Your left hand (or right hand if you're playing a left-handed guitar) will press the strings, and your other hand will strum or pick them.

- Look at the guitar neck – it has metal lines running across it. These are the frets, and the spaces between them are where you press the strings.

- Pick a string to play and gently press it down with the tip of your finger right behind one of the metal frets. Don't press on top of the fret, but just behind it.

- Use enough pressure to make the string touch the guitar's neck.

- Now, with your other hand, pluck the string you're pressing. You've just played a note!

TIP

If the note sounds buzzy or doesn't play, check:

- Is your finger close enough to the fret?
- Are you pressing hard enough?
- Are your other fingers or hand muting the string?

Playing The Guitar

This is the good part, the part I know you've been bursting to get to—playing the guitar!

Calm down, Eddie, or you'll have a little accident again! And I'm not cleaning it up this time!

Notes

Music is made up of sounds, which we call notes. Think of notes as the building blocks of music. Each note has its own unique sound, similar to how we have different colours.

When you play the guitar, each string and fret make a different note. Some notes are high, and some are low. By combining notes, we can play melodies and chords, which make the songs we love!

In music, there are seven main notes: A, B, C, D, E, F, and G.

After G, the notes start again at A, like a musical circle!

There are also "sharp" (#) and "flat" (b) notes, which are like the in-between sounds.

When you learn to play notes on your guitar, you're learning the language of music. Soon, you'll be able to play songs and maybe even write your own!

Fingers

I'm going to ask you to do something now. Get a blank piece of paper and a pencil. Place your left hand on the paper (your right hand if you are playing a left-handed guitar), fingers apart, and draw the outline of your hand. Excellent! Next, I want you to number your fingers, starting with your pinkie finger as number 4, ring finger as number 3, middle finger as number 2, and index finger as number 1. Don't worry about giving your thumb a number; who needs thumbs anyway? Am I right, Eddie?!

Wow, Eddie! Great job! That's excellent! Especially considering giraffes don't have hands!

What is Tuning?

Imagine your guitar is like Eddie and a group of his friends singing. Each string is one of the friends, and they all need to sing the right notes to sound good together. Sometimes, one of the strings might sing too high or too low, causing the whole group to sound "off".

Tuning your guitar means you're helping each string 'sing' the perfect note it's supposed to. You do this by turning the "tuning pegs/machine heads" at the guitar's headstock. Turning the pegs makes the string tighter or looser, which changes how it sounds.

Your guitar sounds fantastic when all the strings sing their notes perfectly! It's like a band of happy friends all singing together in harmony.

How Do We Tune Our Guitar?

There are a few ways to tune your guitar, and you can pick the one that works best for you:

Tuning by Ear

If you're feeling brave, you can tune by listening! You can use another guitar that's already tuned or search for a 'guitar tuning' video online. It'll play the right note for each string, and you can match your guitar to those sounds. If you play another instrument, such as the piano, you can tune using it.

Using a Tuning App or Clip-On Tuner

You can download a free guitar tuning app on a phone or tablet or use a clip-on tuner. These apps and tuners are like magic! When you pluck a string, they listen and tell you if the string is too high, too low, or just right. If the app or tuner says the note is too low, turn the tuning peg to make the string tighter. If it's too high, turn the peg in the opposite direction to make it looser. Do this for each string until they are all perfect! (My favourite app is "GuitarTuna", but there are many options).

Tuning

Chances are, in your eagerness to become a guitar legend, you've already strummed the strings only to find that your guitar sounds like Eddie's stomach after a bad mouthful of acacia leaves. No, your guitar isn't defective. Don't "rage quit" like you do after you lose on your (insert favourite games console here). Speaking of which, you'd better not go back on it until you finish reading this book! Your guitar just needs tuning.

How to Hold the Guitar

Ok, now let's talk about how to hold your guitar. You should have the neck in your left hand (if you are playing a left-handed guitar, this will be the opposite), and the strings should be facing away from your body. I know this might seem obvious to most, but some of us (cough) had to be told repeatedly, didn't we, Eddie?

The back of the guitar should be against your stomach and chest. Keep the neck of the guitar horizontal to the floor.

STRING NAMES

I must be honest with you, Eddie is not the smartest giraffe in the Serengeti. There was an occasion a few years ago when Eddie discovered the remains of a plane crash in which the cargo was explosives! Eddie thought the dynamite, wrapped in a red casing, resembled his favourite chocolate bar. You can guess what he tried to do next... fortunately, I arrived just in time to prevent Eddie from becoming giraffe soup.

That day, we came up with an acronym to remind Eddie that the consequences of eating explosives are not good! And, by purely happy coincidence, that same acronym is a perfect way to remember the string names on the guitar!

Starting from the low E, (the string at the top of the guitar)...

(LOW) **E**ddie
Ate
Dynamite
Good
Bye
(HIGH) **E**ddie

Fantastic!
Now that we know one another, we can get started!

Now, I'm not going to lie to you and tell you that once you're finished reading this book, you're going to be a complete guitar virtuoso like Goose Springsteen or Jimmi Hen-drix, but you will be able to play a little something and have a solid base to begin your guitar journey.

THIS IS EDDIE

Eddie is a giraffe. A giraffe who just so happens to play the guitar. With Eddie's help, after you have read these pages, you will be able to play the guitar too!

Say Hi Eddie!

Now, come on, I know you didn't say hi. You read it, but you didn't actually say it!

SHOUT Hi Eddie!

Giraffes are really tall, it's a long way up to their ears, and Eddie is hard of hearing.

The moral rights of the author have been asserted

All rights reserved

No part of this publication maybe reproduced, stored in a retrieval system or transmitted in any form or by any means, without the prior permission in writing of the publisher or the author, nor be otherwise circulated in any form of binding or cover other than that in which it is published and without a similar condition including this condition being imposed on the subsequent purchaser.

Name : Parker Publishers
Address: UK: 71-75 Shelton Street, Covent Garden, London, WC2H 9JQ

www.parkerpublishers.co.uk
Our books may be purchased in bulk for promotional, educational, or business use.
Please contact [Parker Publishers] at [020 4579 4589], or by email at [info@parkerpublishers.co.uk]

First Edition 2025
ISBN:
Ebook : 9781918199031
Paperback: 9781918199048
Hardback: 978-1-918199-05-5